THREE TACTICS

The
Background
in
Marx

THREE TACTICS

The Background in Marx

by
STANLEY MOORE

Monthly Review Press
New York 1963

CONTENTS

PREFACE

The immediate occasion for these essays was a friendly argument with Leo Huberman and Paul Sweezy over the significance of the current disputes among Russian, Chinese, and Yugoslavian Communists. In the course of our discussion I promised to write for MONTHLY REVIEW a series of articles attempting to clarify certain theoretical aspects of these controversies. That was in May of 1962. During the following months I produced three essays, pointing to the tensions and conflicts in Marx's doctrines which provide a theoretical component for the tactical quarrels that periodically divide his followers.

I submitted my manuscript at the beginning of this year. After reading it the editors of MONTHLY REVIEW—who happen also to head Monthly Review Press—suggested that my discussion, instead of being chopped up for magazine publication, be presented in the form of a short book. Their proposal was accepted, and this is the result.

In shifting to a different form of publication I have made no changes in the original essays. I have persisted in my first intention, which was to state an hypothesis rather than to confirm one, to suggest rather than to exhaust. These essays are designed as a scaffolding from which to work, not as a building in which to live.

STANLEY MOORE

New York City
February 1963

MARX
AND
MINORITY
REVOLUTION

1

Quarrels over tactics, centering on the relation of reform to revolution, have divided the socialist movement established by Marx and Engels during each generation since the death of its founders. At the turn of the century, this debate separated adherents of revisionism from adherents of orthodoxy within the Social Democratic parties. Between the two world wars, it was a central feature of the conflict between Social Democrats and Communists. Since then, in struggles between Tito and Stalin, Khrushchev and Mao, it has been reborn inside the Communist movement. An Hegelian, viewing this series of disputes as a process of development through contradiction, might find in the opposition of reform and revolution a key to the dialectic of Marxism.

These conflicts seem to exhibit a striking continuity, an opposition of policies and theories which has persisted in the face of radically changing historical conditions. When the first debate over revisionism broke out among Bernstein, Kautsky, and Luxemburg, what was the situation of the socialist movement? Bolsheviks had not separated from Mensheviks. Socialist parties, almost without exception, were confined to Europe and America. In no country of the world were socialists in power. And now, after sixty years, after two world wars, after the Russian Revolution and the

11

Chinese Revolution, what are Tito, Khrushchev, and Mao debating? We are told that the issue is revisionism.

It can be argued that this continuity is spurious. An insistence upon stating current problems in the categories of dead authorities and upon describing current situations in terms of historical analogies can be expected to result in continuities that are purely verbal. As a word like revisionism is stretched to cover increasingly different problems and situations, it may be drained of all determinate reference and degraded into a simple term of abuse.

Or it can be argued that even if the continuity is genuine, it is nevertheless misleading. Suppose that at some level of abstraction some degree of continuity could be discovered between the tactics proposed by one of the currently disputing groups, one of the groups disputing between the two world wars, and one of the groups disputing at the opening of the century. Would it follow that all were equally right or equally wrong? To the extent that historical conditions change, policies correct at one time become incorrect at another. In discussing tactics, the decisive comparison is not with past tactics but with present facts.

Finally it can be argued that even in Marxian politics tactical disputes are seldom primarily concerned with abstract principles. At the superficial level they reflect that competition for leadership, between contending personalities backed by contending groups, which accompanies all political activity. And beneath that level the issues turn largely upon differences of judgement. Contestants disagree in their beliefs concerning the facts of the situation and in their estimates of the risks entailed by alternative lines of action.

To the extent that theoretical principles are involved, it is not conflicting theories that confront one another but conflicting applications of the same theory.

Granted the force of all three lines of argument, do they bar an attempt to trace some aspects of the current dispute to their antecedents in Marxian theory? I look on these arguments, not as prohibitions, but as cautions. I admit that tracing the theoretical ancestry of this dispute is only one of many ways to approach it. And I admit that this approach, taken by itself, cannot decide which of the contending policies best fits the facts of the current situation. But though backing away from the target in this fashion cannot provide answers, it may clarify questions; and for understanding a conflict where pronouncement and abuse so often take the place of reasoned argument, such clarification is urgently required.

Socialist disputes over tactics raise theoretical issues to the extent that opposing policies assume, explicitly or implicitly, contrasting patterns of transition from capitalism to socialism. Of course, to raise a theoretical problem, more must be involved than the application of a single consistent theory to widely different sets of circumstances. The contrast must include a conflict of principles.

In these essays I propose to show that three such contrasting patterns, or alternative models, can be discovered in what Marx wrote concerning the transition from capitalism to socialism. They can be nicknamed the pattern of permanent revolution, the pattern of increasing misery, and the pattern of competing systems. After distinguishing and comparing these models, I shall attempt to relate them at their points of conflict to the tactical disputes that have so persistently divided Marxian socialists.

2

Marx announced his conversion from radical democrat into philosophical communist with an essay on the pre-requisites for a proletarian revolution in a backward country. The essay was his *Introduction to a Critique of Hegel's Philosophy of Right*, which he published early in 1844. The backward country was Germany, which at that time lagged as decisively behind England and France, both politically and economically, as in 1917 Russia lagged behind Western Europe.

Germany, Marx writes, has not experienced a bourgeois revolution: it has shared in the reaction produced by the French Revolution without sharing in the revolution itself. But a bourgeois revolution is impossible for Germany. Her capitalists lack both the capacity and the desire to unite under their leadership all social groups opposed to feudalism, to emancipate themselves by overthrowing the existing order in the name of emancipating society. There can be no bourgeois revolution without a revolutionary bourgeoisie.

But though Germany cannot attain the stage of political development already reached by France and England, it can skip that stage. A proletarian revolution is possible, although a bourgeois revolution is impossible. "It is not the radical revolution, the general human emancipation, that is a utopian dream for Germany: it is rather the partial, the merely political revolution, the revolution that leaves standing the pillars of the building."

What circumstances make possible this radical revolution? The first prerequisite is a revolutionary theory. Germans are philosophical contemporaries of the French and English without being their political or economic contemporaries. German theory has provided a radical critique of institutions to which German society has not yet progressed. The second prerequisite is a revolutionary class. The incipient industrialization of Germany is producing a class of wage-workers which cannot emancipate itself without emancipating all society, in fact as well as in name. This class finds in revolutionary theory the answer to its radical needs. "Philosophy is the head of this emancipation: its heart is the proletariat."

Viewed from the standpoint of Marx's *Capital*, this discussion of the prospects for a proletarian revolution in a backward country raises more questions than it answers. Did Marx expect the revolution to occur only when German industrialization had reached the level that England and France had already attained in 1844? Then, since it was reasonable to suppose that this advance would require decades, how could he believe that throughout this period it would be impossible for the capitalists to attain political as well as economic rule? Or did Marx expect the revolution in the immediate future, with German industrialization at approximately its current level? How then could he believe that it would be possible for his proposed alliance of philosophers and proletarians—a small fraction of the total population—to overthrow the existing political order and take over the task of industrializing Germany?

Such questions, however, are at least in part products of hindsight, for Marx's essay was not written from the standpoint of *Capital*. His study of French revolutionary politics and British political economy commenced with his move to Paris, only a few months before publication of his *Introduction to a Critique of Hegel's Philosophy of Right*. That essay, though it reflects the impact of these new ideas, represents the beginning of a protracted process of assimilation and development. The evidence indicates that its discussion of the contrasting prospects for a partial and a radical revolution is less an attempt to develop an original theory than an attempt to apply to German conditions a theory already at hand. The contrast between a merely political and a social revolution was central for a tradition of revolutionary socialism that was nearly fifty years old when Marx encountered it in Paris. This tradition had been established in 1796 by members of the Conspiracy of the Equals, led by Babeuf and Buonarroti. Among the contemporaries of Marx, its principal inheritors were members of the Society of the Seasons, led by Barbès and Blanqui.

3

Buonarroti's *History of Babeuf's Conspiracy for Equality* is not simply a narrative of an abortive insurrection. In attempting to explain and justify that insurrection, Buonarroti expounds in detail its principles, program, organization, and tactics. The major contribution of his book is its description of the first systematic plan for carrying out a socialist revolution. In the light of subsequent disputes over socialist tactics, three related aspects of that plan are of particular significance: the doctrine of unfinished revolution, the doctrine of minority rule, and the doctrine of conspiratorial leadership.

Buonarroti's interpretation of the French Revolution centers upon the conflict between advocates of two different types of revolution. One set of revolutionaries aimed simply at a change in the form of government which would substitute the rule of a new minority for that of the old, an aristocracy of wealth for that of blood. These Buonarroti calls the partisans of egoism. The other set of revolutionaries had more radical aims: they sought not only the replacement of all minority rule by democracy but a complete reform of society in the interests of the great majority. These Buonarroti calls the partisans of equality.

Throughout the early years of the revolution, he writes, partisans of egoism were in power. Then the ascendancy of Robespierre marked the triumph of the partisans of equality. The principal achievements of the Jacobin period were the democratic constitution of 1793 and the social reforms adopted under the leadership of the Committee of Public Safety. Then Thermidor marked the overthrow of the partisans of equality, and under the Directory partisans of egoism established once again an aristocracy of wealth. In this situation Babeuf organized the Conspiracy of the Equals. Its aim was to overthrow the Directory, in order to complete the unfinished revolution.

The program of Babeuf and Buonarroti was not, however, a reaffirmation of Jacobin equalitarianism. They praised the Constitution of 1793 for proclaiming the sovereignty of the people, while criticizing it for recognizing private property as a natural right. They praised the reforms introduced as emergency measures during the war against foreign intervention, while denying the efficacy of such reforms for permanently securing social equality. Instead of redistributing private property, they proposed to abolish it and to organize in its place a community of goods and labour. To complete the revolution it was necessary to establish, not only a democratic state, but a socialist economy.

Were these two aims compatible in the France of 1796? While contending that abolition of private property would be to the interest of the great majority, the conspirators recognized that only a few of that majority agreed with them. "The Committee," writes Buonarroti concerning the leaders of the insurrection, "did not conceal from themselves how harmful to morality and the common cause had been the catastrophe of 9 Thermidor and the tragic events which followed. They knew that a multitude of citizens had reacted by abandoning themselves to the most disgraceful rapacity. They recognized that even the smallest proprietors, who shortly before had been ready to renounce their possessions, were now once more attached to them, convinced that legislation had lost all consideration for the common good and had been abandoned to the most unrestrained egoism." Under these circumstances, to give the majority what they wanted would be to deny them what they needed. Until the new society could be firmly established and its members taught by experience to recognize their common interest, it would be necessary to choose between democracy and socialism.

Faced with this situation, the conspirators agreed that the conflict could be resolved only in the course of an extended period of minority rule. Their immediate task was to overthrow the existing government. Their ultimate task was to establish a government operating within the framework of a democratic constitution. An intermediate task was to organize a provisional government, acting in the interest of the majority but not controlled by the majority, aiming at establishment of a constitution but unrestrained by law. Some conspirators proposed that this transitional government should take the form of a dictatorship, which they defined as extraordinary authority entrusted to a single man. But the plan that was adopted called for a small governing body of tested revolutionaries, to be elected by the insurgents of Paris after nomination by the committee directing the conspiracy.

Babeuf's preparations for the insurrection provide a classical example of conspiratorial leadership. All decisions came from a Directory of Public Safety, secret and self-appointed, consisting of seven men. This committee appointed a revolutionary agent for each of the twelve districts of Paris and five additional agents for the military forces in the area. Acting on detailed instructions from the directory and reporting back to it, each agent undertook to spread propaganda for the conspiracy, including newspapers and leaflets, and also to organize groups of activists, provided as far as possible with arms. The aims of this preparatory activity were, first, to create a popular army capable of overcoming any military forces that remained loyal to the old government, and second, to rally the multitude of working people in support of the insurrection. When the leaders gave the word to act, the first step would be to seize stores of munitions and the major government offices. The second step would be to decree immediate provision of food and housing for the poor. And the third step would be to organize a revolutionary government.

When the members of the provisional authority had been nominated and elected, would the Directory of Public Safety then dissolve? Buonarroti reports that the leaders' discussion of this delicate point was inconclusive. They almost decided to demand from the people a decree entrusting them with exclusive authority to propose and execute the laws. They did decide that at the very least their committee should remain in existence to supervise the work of the elected officials. The last article of the Proclamation of Insurrection states that the directory shall continue in existence until the task of the insurrection has been wholly completed.

4

After its publication in 1828 Buonarroti's *History* became the guide for an entire generation of revolutionaries, among whom the most notable was Blanqui. Before discussing the influence of this tradition upon Marx, it is useful to indicate the extent to which Blanqui elaborated and modified the doctrines of unfinished revolution, minority rule, and conspiratorial leadership.

To a greater extent than Babeuf or Buonarroti, Blanqui interpreted the doctrine of unfinished revolution in terms of a struggle between classes. For their general contrast between rich and poor he tended to substitute the more specific contrast between bourgeoisie and proletariat. Though his definition of the proletariat lacked theoretical precision, his tactics effectively distinguished the political role of the wage-workers from that of the peasants and that of the petty bourgeoisie. Establishment of a democratic constitution was an ultimate goal: but the immediate task of the revolution was to bring, not the majority, but the wage-workers to power.

Blanqui presented the doctrine of minority rule in terms of a collective dictatorship. In the France of his time, he believed, a revolutionary dictatorship should involve rule by the majority in Paris and rule by Paris over the majority in France. Accordingly, during the Revolution of 1848 he strongly opposed an immediate appeal to universal suffrage. Reaffirming this position from the vantage point of 1870, he wrote in the last chapter of his *Capital et Travail*: "The hasty appeal to universal suffrage in 1848 was a deliberate betrayal. The politicians knew that, due to the gagging of the press throughout the years since Napoleon's seizure of power, the provinces had become the prey of the priests, the bureaucrats, and the aristocrats. To ask for the vote of this enslaved population was to ask for the vote of its masters. . . . In 1848, one year of the dictatorship of Paris would have spared France the events of the quarter-century now drawing to its close. If this time ten years are required, we should not hesitate." Proletarian dictatorship is the last historical form of minority rule.

In his doctrine of conspiratorial organization Blanqui elaborated the basic pattern established by Babeuf and Buonarroti. But he significantly altered their analysis of the sources of revolutionary leadership, substituting for their moralistic account—centered upon the contrast between the virtuous and the corrupt—one that was more sociological in

approach. An effective conspiratorial organization, he believed, would unite the most radical members of the proletariat under the guidance of the most radical members of
the declassed bourgeois intelligentsia.

It is sometimes claimed that Blanqui, obsessed with
conspiracy and the mechanics of the *coup d'état*, neglected
propaganda and the task of organizing the entire working
class to carry out the revolution. This criticism may apply to
his leadership of the insurrection attempted by the Society of
the Seasons in 1839. But it does not apply to his leadership
in the Revolution of 1848. On his return from prison at
the start of that revolution he organized, not a secret society, but an open propagandist club. In the existing circumstances he opposed insurrection, advocating instead the
arming of all workers in Paris. What was required to push
the revolution forward, he insisted, was not a surprise attack
but the concerted action of a class in arms.

5

From the beginning of 1844, when Marx and Engels
announced their conversion to communism, until the end of
1850, when they faced the fact that the crisis of 1848 was
over, their revolutionary tactics were primarily influenced by
the tradition of Babeuf, Buonarroti, and Blanqui. This tradition was not the only influence on Marx and Engels. They
were far from accepting its principles uncritically. Yet the
key to understanding their tactics during this period is to

examine the position they adopted on the doctrines of permanent revolution, proletarian dictatorship, and conspiratorial leadership.

The slogan of permanent revolution does not appear in the *Communist Manifesto*. But the concept is implicit in the claim that Germany is on the eve of a bourgeois revolution that will be immediately followed by a proletarian revolution. After the successes of 1848 and the defeats of 1849, Marx and Engels, in the *First Address of the Central Committee of the Communist League to its Members in Germany,* presented a detailed tactical plan for carrying forward the revolution. In this address they distinguish three political programs, representing three classes struggling to dominate the revolution: bourgeois Liberalism, petty-bourgeois Democracy, and proletarian Communism. Throughout every stage of revolutionary development the proletarians must build their independent organization and present their independent program. But at each new stage they must shift their alliances and increase their demands. During the period when bourgeois Liberals are in the ascendancy, Communists should support the struggle of petty-bourgeois Democrats to take power. But in the period when petty-bourgeois Democrats are in the ascendancy, Communists should struggle to replace them. These tactics are summarized in the statement that the battle-cry of the proletariat must be "The Permanent Revolution."

The slogan of proletarian dictatorship does not appear in the *Communist Manifesto*. What is more, the necessity for minority rule seems denied by the claim that the proletariat will become the ruling class through winning the battle for democracy. This claim seems reasonable for a country where proletarians are in the majority. But what about countries where this is not the case? Engels attempts to answer this question in his *Principles of Communism,* the preliminary draft he wrote for the *Manifesto.* He asserts there that establishment of a democratic constitution will "directly or indirectly" entail political rule by the proletariat. It will do so directly in England, where proletarians already constitute a majority of the population. It will do so indirectly in France and Germany, where proletarians are not in the majority. There the peasants and petty bourgeoisie are being transformed into proletarians. They will accordingly be impelled by their political interests towards increasing dependence on the proletariat. They must then accommodate themselves to the proletariat's demands. Engels adds that "perhaps" this will require a second struggle, which will end in the victory of the proletariat. But if such a second struggle occurs, it might be asked, would not this victory amount to triumph of a minority over the majority, replacement of petty-bourgeois democracy by proletarian dictatorship?

The revolutions of 1848, in both France and Germany, convinced Marx and Engels that this second struggle was not merely possible but unavoidable. In their judgement Germany, after the overthrow of its feudal-bureaucratic governments, entered the stage of struggle for democracy. The immediate task of proletarian Communists was to join petty-bourgeois Democrats in opposing bourgeois Liberals. But, Marx and Engels prophesied in their *First Address to the Communist League,* during the next stage Communists would oppose petty-bourgeois Democrats. In France, on the other hand, a section of the bourgeoisie had been in power before the revolution; and developments during the first few months raised problems of the second stage, of struggle for proletarian dictatorship. The history of this period Marx analyzed in *The Class Struggles in France*. He wrote there that when in June of 1848 petty-bourgeois Democrats joined bourgeois Liberals to crush the proletariat, their victims learned the consequences of the appeal to universal suffrage. Proletarians then replaced their modest demands for reform with the battle-cry of revolutionary struggle: "Overthrow of the Bourgeoisie! Dictatorship of the Working Class!" From Marx's statement in the same work that the majority of Frenchmen were peasants, it follows that this was a demand for minority rule.

6

During the years from 1844 through 1850, it was the doctrine of conspiratorial leadership that most sharply separated the tactical theories of Marx and Engels from the tradition of Babeuf, Buonarroti, and Blanqui. Yet, viewed within the historical context of this period and without reference to later developments, their disagreements seem rather differences of emphasis within a single movement than differences of principle between two competing movements.

In *Der Sozialismus in Deutschland* Engels gives an account of the sources of revolutionary leadership quite similar to that of Blanqui. "At the beginning," he writes, "there were two independent movements. On the one hand, a pure workers' movement, deriving from French communist workers:

the utopian communism of Weitling represents a stage of its development. On the other hand, a theoretical movement, resulting from the dissolution of Hegel's philosophy: this group was dominated from the very first by Marx. The *Communist Manifesto* of January 1848 represents the unification of the two movements, a unification completed in the struggles of the revolution where both the workers and the ex-philosophers fought with courage." The record shows that this unification was not accomplished without conflict. Weitling opposed Marx's bid for leadership, on the ground that intellectuals were not appropriate leaders for a workers' movement.

Who were the French communists that inspired the German workers' movement? In his essay *On the History of the Communist League,* Engels writes that the communism of the French workers derived from the tradition of Babeuf. He reports further that the League of the Just—the organization started in Paris by German workers which a decade later became the Communist League—was at the time of its formation in 1836 little more than a German branch of the Society of the Seasons, led by Barbès and Blanqui. In the unsuccessful insurrection of 1839 members of the two organizations fought side by side.

After this defeat, Engels continues, the center of the League shifted to London and its activities lost some of their conspiratorial character. An open organization, the German Workers' Educational Association, was established to serve as a forum for propaganda and a source of recruits. The last stage in the development of the League from an organization of conspirators into an organization of propagandists was reached in 1847, when its members marked their acceptance of the leadership of Marx and Engels by reconstituting their organization as the Communist League.

What did the shift from conspiracy to propaganda involve? One consequence was less secrecy. The League continued the policy of concealing its membership from the police. But it rejected the principle of isolating its members from one another, that is, of building a pyramid rising from small groups in each of which only the organizer had contact with a higher level, through successive levels of command also organized on the principle of minimum contact, to leaders unknown to the membership at large. Another consequence was more democracy. The League continued to restrict its membership to the most advanced adherents of the workers' movement. But in its internal structure the conspiratorial principle of appointment from above was replaced by the democratic principle of election from below.

It would be a mistake, however, to discover in these changes a definitive rupture with the principles of Blanqui. In the first place, Blanqui too was prepared, in some situations, to abandon tactics of conspiracy for those of open propaganda. In the second place, the significance of these changes in the structure of the League must be weighed against the significance of its new name. Marx and Engels had not raised the spectre that was haunting Europe in 1848. At that period, as Marx points out in *The Class Struggles in France*, the bourgeoisie identified communism with Blanqui. For the predominantly German-speaking League to call itself communist was to affirm publicly its solidarity with the French followers of Blanqui.

Two years of experience as revolutionary leaders brought Marx and Engels still closer to the movement headed by

Blanqui. At the start of the German revolution Marx dissolved the Communist League. Open workers' organizations existed in major cities: open propaganda could be carried on through the *Neue Rheinische Zeitung*. In the circumstances a secret propaganda society seemed superfluous. Yet two years later both the open workers' organizations and the *Neue Rheinische Zeitung* had been destroyed by the counterrevolution; and, in their first address to the members of the reconstituted League, Marx and Engels in effect admitted that its dissolution had been a mistake. They now assigned to the League more than a purely educational function. In their second address to the members they asserted that its aim was to organize a revolutionary workers' party in Germany. At the same time, as representatives of the League, they united in a secret society with representatives of the French followers of Blanqui.

The *Société Universelle des Communistes Révolutionnaires* was established in London during April of 1850. Its statutes were signed by three representatives of the Communist League (including Marx and Engels), two representatives of Blanquist organizations in exile, and one representative of the Chartists. The association was restricted to leaders. Not only its membership but its existence was kept secret from the rank and file. The first paragraph of its statutes states: "The aim of the association is to overthrow the privileged classes, to subject them to the dictatorship of the proletariat, and to continue the permanent revolution until the attainment of communism, which shall be the ultimate form of human society."

This was the point of greatest unity—doctrinal and organizational—between Marx and Blanqui. Within a few months Marx and Engels decided that the revolutionary crisis was over and the secret association dead. They were never as close to Blanqui again.

7

To point out Marx's debt to the tradition of Babeuf, Buonarroti, and Blanqui is to consider only one of the major currents in his intellectual development. During the years from 1844 through 1850, this tradition was the principal source for his model of the transition from capitalism to socialism and, consequently, for his tactical doctrines. Yet throughout this period he studied, not only French revolutionary politics, but also British political economy; and the interaction of these influences produced a latent conflict between his tactical doctrines and the basic principles of historical materialism. This conflict foreshadowed a turning away, in the years after 1850, from the pattern of permanent revolution to other models of the transition from capitalism to socialism.

The problem of the connection between tactical doctrines and historical approach is raised by Marx's strongest affirmation of theoretical solidarity with Blanqui. The communism of Blanqui, he writes in *The Class Struggles in France,* is "the declaration of the permanence of the revolution, the class dictatorship of the proletariat as the necessary transition to abolition of all class differences, to abolition of all relations of production on which these differences rest,

to abolition of the totality of social relations corresponding
to these relations of production, and to the revolutionizing
of all ideas arising from these social relations." The first
part of this description points to a theory of revolution, the
last part to a theory of history. Undeniably Marx and
Blanqui shared at that time the doctrines of class struggle,
permanent revolution, and proletarian dictatorship. Did they
also share the theory of productive forces and relations, the
theory of the primacy of economic change in social development, and the theory of the primacy of social existence over
social consciousness? Or does the Marxian approach to
history differ decisively from that represented by Blanqui?

Such a difference is at least suggested by the attacks
of Marx and Engels upon the professional conspirator's approach to politics. On the ignorance of social theory pre-
valent in conspiratorial organizations, Engels wrote, in his
essay *On the History of the Communist League,* that he believed not a single member of the League of the Just had
ever read a book on political economy. The words "equality,"
"brotherhood," and "justice" provided solutions for all theoretical difficulties. On the refusal to recognize social facts
characteristic of conspiratorial leaders, Marx and Engels
wrote, in a review of two books about French conspirators
during the era of 1848: "These conspirators do not confine
themselves to organizing the revolutionary proletariat. Their
occupation consists in forestalling the process of revolutionary
development, spurring it on to artificial crises, making revolutions extempore without the conditions for revolution.
For them the only condition required for the revolution is
sufficient organization of their own conspiracy. They are
the alchemists of revolution . . ." At the close of 1850 the

insistence of Marx and Engels that the end of the economic crisis marked the end of the revolutionary crisis, and that another economic crisis was a necessary condition for another revolution, caused their final break with the followers of Blanqui. To the extent that Blanqui shared the defects of his followers, his approach to politics clashed with the outlook of historical materialism.

These criticisms can be summarized in the charge that the conspiratorial approach exaggerates the potentialities of political action, neglecting the limitations imposed upon such action by objective conditions in general and by economic factors in particular. But how far should this line of argument be pursued? Could not the same criticism apply to the plan of Marx and Engels for a proletarian revolution in a backward country?

Stating the viewpoint of historical materialism in the Preface to his *Critique of Political Economy,* Marx writes: "No social order ever disappears before all the productive forces it has room for have been developed. New, higher relations of production never appear before the material conditions of their existence have matured in the womb of the old society." Are these principles consistent with a program calling for uninterrupted development from a bourgeois to a proletarian revolution, for socialist completion of an industrialization that capitalists have barely begun? Does not the pattern of permanent revolution, taken as a model for the transition from capitalism to socialism, share the major defects of the conspiratorial approach to history?

During the remainder of Marx's lifetime this conflict was not so much resolved as obscured. German history took a course quite different from that prophesied by the *Mani-*

festo, following a pattern which Engels analyzed—after the
establishment of Bismarck's Empire—in his theory of bourgeois revolution from above. The development of Marx's
economic thought, culminating in *Capital,* shifted the focus
of attention to problems of proletarian revolution in a developed capitalist society, one where the process of capital
accumulation has largely succeeded in splitting the economy
into a small minority of capitalists and a large majority of
proletarians. The tactical doctrines of the Marxian movement shifted in their assumptions from the pattern of permanent revolution to another model for the transition from
capitalism to socialism, the pattern of increasing misery.

But Germany was not the last backward country in
Europe. During the years after Engels' death, Lenin adapted
and elaborated for Russia the tactical doctrines Marx had
developed for Germany during the years from 1844 through
1850. After the Bolshevik Revolution, the polemics of Lenin
and Kautsky marked the transformation of a latent tension
in Marx's thought into an open confrontation of hostile
political movements. Both Lenin and Kautsky claimed to in-
herit Marx's teaching, but they appealed to different parts of
it. Neither was prepared to admit the full complexity of that
inheritance.

Lenin and his adherents could appeal to the *Communist
Manifesto* on the historical destiny of Germany. "The Communists turn their attention chiefly to Germany, because that
country is on the eve of a bourgeois revolution that is bound
to be carried out under more advanced conditions of European
civilization, and with a much more developed proletariat,
than the bourgeois revolution of England in the seventeenth
century or that of France in the eighteenth century, and be-

cause therefore this bourgeois revolution can be but the prelude to an immediately following proletarian revolution." Did not this explain how the Bolsheviks had taken power?

Kautsky and his adherents could point to the actual history of Germany and appeal to the *Communist Manifesto* on Babeuf. "The first direct attempts of the proletariat to attain its own ends, made in times of general upheaval when feudal society was being overthrown, necessarily failed, owing to the undeveloped state of the proletariat and the absence of the economic conditions for its emancipation—conditions that had yet to be produced, and could only be produced, by the impending capitalist epoch." Did not this explain why, though the Bolsheviks had taken power, the proletariat could not rule?

MARX
AND
MAJORITY
REVOLUTION

1

In his early writings on socialist tactics, during the period from 1844 through 1850, Marx dealt mainly with the relation of proletarian communism to bourgeois liberalism and petty-bourgeois democracy. In this period he concentrated primarily upon Germany, secondarily upon France. His later writings on tactics fall into two groups. During the period of the First International, from 1864 through 1872, he dealt mainly with the relation of the trade-union movement to the socialist movement. In this period he concentrated primarily upon England, secondarily upon France. During the remaining years before his death in 1883, he dealt mainly with the role of a socialist party in a capitalist state where the working class could vote. In this period he concentrated primarily upon Germany, secondarily upon France.

The tactical writings before 1850 are separated from those after 1864 by more than the temporal gap of fourteen years. In the first place, Marx's intensive study of British political economy was very largely concentrated in those intervening years. Before 1850 he had produced in the field of economic theory only his attack on Proudhon and the popular lectures *Wage-Labour and Capital*. By the end of 1865 he had published his *Critique of Political Economy* and had completed the rough drafts for all three volumes of *Capital*. In the second place, the practical problems he dealt with in his later years differed radically from those he had confronted as leader of the Communist League. The Germany of 1848 Marx considered, even for that time, a backward country. Economically it was in the first stages of industrialization; politically it was at the point of bourgeois revolution. The England of 1864 Marx considered the most advanced of capitalist countries. Industrialization had reached the point where wage-workers constituted a majority of the population. The economic successes of trade unionism had organized support for a political movement that was shortly to extend the franchise to the working class. In spite of important differences, economic and political, Marx saw the same basic forces at work in France: industrialization producing the conditions for trade unionism, trade unionism producing the conditions for a socialist movement. And when, after the decline of the International, he focused his attention once more on Germany, he saw there a comparable situation. Obviously there were major differences between conditions in Bismarck's Empire and those in contemporary France or England. But the tactical problems of the socialist movement in the Germany of 1875 were far more similar to those in England and France than to those in the Germany of 1848.

Both shifts of emphasis, theoretical and practical, pointed in the same direction. The practical problem was to work out a general tactical plan for a socialist movement in an industrialized capitalist society. The theoretical solution was to base this plan on a model of the transition from capitalism to socialism built around the law of capitalist accumulation. This development did not involve a sharp break in the continuity of Marxian theory: the problem had been stated and the solution indicated as early as the *Communist Manifesto*. What it did involve was a shift in emphasis from one aspect of that theory to another, from the pattern of permanent revolution to the pattern of increasing misery.

The pattern of increasing misery is the most complex and fully developed of Marx's models for the transition from capitalism to socialism. It involves a theory of capitalist accumulation, a theory of class-consciousness, and a theory of state power. The relevant theses of the theory of capitalist accumulation are, first, that industrialization increasingly divides an economy into a small minority of capitalists and a large majority of wage-workers, second, that industrialization forces these wage-workers into lives of increasing misery. The relevant theses of the theory of class-consciousness are, first, that industrialization fosters growth of a trade-union movement, second, that growth of a trade-union movement fosters growth of a socialist movement. The relevant theses of the theory of state power are, first, that the socialist movement can make use of representative institutions in a capitalist state to organize and educate the working class, second, that even though socialists attain an electoral majority, peaceful transition to a socialist economy will be blocked—under normal conditions—by armed resistance of a minority. It is a pattern of majority revolution.

2

The thesis of class polarization is stated repeatedly in the *Communist Manifesto,* and its significance for revolutionary tactics is clearly indicated. "Of all the classes that confront the bourgeoisie today, the proletariat alone is a really revolutionary class. The other classes decay and disappear with the growth of large-scale industry: the proletariat is its distinctive product." Twenty years later Marx quoted this passage, summarizing, at the climax of the first volume of *Capital,* the historical tendency of capitalist accumulation. After another eight years he quoted it once more, discussing, in his *Critique of the Gotha Program*, the tactics of the newly formed Social Democratic Party of Germany. The polarization thesis was affirmed, without even a change of wording, in all three of the periods during which he wrote on tactics.

Is the thesis of class polarization a flat prediction? Or is it merely the claim that capitalist accumulation exhibits a certain tendency, which may or may not be outweighed by counteracting tendencies? At some points in his writings Marx seems to define proletarians as wage-workers of a particular kind, those who participate directly in the production of material objects. During the course of capitalist development, he asserts in the first volume of *Capital* and in the first volume of his *Theorien über den Mehrwert*, the ratio of such productive workers to all wage-workers progressively declines. If proletarians are distinguished from other wage-workers in this fashion, then transformation of the majority of the population into wage-workers is not equivalent to transformation of this majority into proletarians. But this distinction is not drawn in any of Marx's tactical writings, or in the section of *Capital* dealing with the historical tendency of capitalist accumulation. There proletarian revolution is characterized as expropriation of a small minority, the capitalists and landlords, by an overwhelming majority, the wage-workers.

The thesis of increasing misery, as formulated in the *Communist Manifesto,* asserts that the lives of proletarians grow more miserable in three respects. First, their work becomes increasingly repulsive—more strenuous, more monotonous, more despotically controlled. Second, their employment becomes increasingly insecure. And third, their real wages progressively decline. Reformulating this thesis in his chapter on the general law of capitalist accumulation, near the end of the first volume of *Capital,* Marx asserts a progressive increase in repulsiveness of work and insecurity of employment. But he no longer asserts a progressive lowering of wages. In his *Critique of the Gotha Program* he reaffirms the thesis in this modified form.

Is the thesis of increasing misery a flat prediction? Or is it merely the claim that capitalist accumulation exhibits a certain tendency, which may or may not be outweighed by counteracting tendencies? In the chapter in the first volume of *Capital* on the general law of capitalist accumulation—which contains his most detailed and systematic presentation of the thesis—Marx seems to offer some support for the second interpretation. After stating as the "absolute general law" of capitalist accumulation the proposition that accumulation increases the ratio of unemployed to employed members of the labor force, he adds: "Like all other laws it is modified in its working by many circumstances, but these are not relevant to our present analysis." Could such modifying circumstances produce a situation where the tendency toward increasing misery is balanced or outweighed?

Marx gives a negative answer, for the long run at least, in the crucial section of the first volume of *Capital* where he outlines the historical tendency of capitalist accumulation.

He asserts there that capitalist production gives rise "with the inexorability of a law of nature" to its negation—that is, to socialist society established through proletarian revolution. And in this passage his decisive premise for predicting a proletarian revolution is his prediction of increasing misery. To concede that in a capitalist society increasing misery could remain a tendency, without ever becoming an actuality, would be to abandon the central argument of *Capital*. Without a flat prediction how could Marx hope to demonstrate, from the law of motion of capitalist society, the inevitability of proletarian revolution?

Surveying in his *Inaugural Address* the period from 1848 to the establishment of the International, Marx does not assert that misery has increased but he denies that it has declined. He commences with a categorical statement: "It is a great fact that the misery of the working masses has not diminished from 1848 to 1864, and yet this period is unrivalled for the development of its industry and the growth of its commerce." In England and the other industrial countries of Europe, he admits, real wages rose during this period for a minority of the working class. Yet "the great mass of the working classes were sinking down to a lower depth, at the same rate at least, that those above them were rising in the social scale." In all countries of Europe, he concludes, it has now been demonstrated that no improvement of machinery, no application of science to production, no new colonies, no opening of markets, can do away with the miseries of the working class.

Eleven years afterward, in his *Critique of the Gotha Program*, Marx restated the thesis of increasing misery in sweeping terms. It is a law of all history up to the present, he asserts, that "In proportion as labour develops socially and becomes thereby a source of wealth and culture, poverty and deprivation develop among the workers, wealth and culture among the non-workers." The task of the socialist program, he concludes, is to show how in contemporary capitalist society the conditions have been created which enable and compel the workers to end this evil.

3

Class polarization and increasing misery create the need for proletarian revolution. But how does the working class become conscious of this need? The first phase in recognition of the problem and creation of agencies for its solution is growth of a trade-union movement. The second is growth of a socialist party.

The Marxian position on the connection between trade unionism and class-consciousness is outlined in the *Communist Manifesto*. Trade unions, it is asserted there, are formed in the course of struggles over wages. But such struggles are no more than temporarily successful in attaining their immediate aim. Their cumulative gain is increasing organization of the working class.

During the era of the First International, Marx restated these views in a resolution he wrote for its Geneva Congress. The resolution claims that trade unions, without being aware of the fact, have become centers for the organization of the workers as a class. Indispensable for defensive struggles over

wages and hours against the economic power of the em-
ployers, they are even more important as a force for overthrowing the entire system of wage labour and capitalist rule.

The second phase in the organization and education of
the working class is growth of a socialist party. The *Communist Manifesto* asserts that the workers' economic struggle
develops into political struggle, that their organization as a
class through the growth of trade unions results in their
organization as a political party. As an example of political
struggle growing out of economic struggle, Marx and Engels
cite the role of the English trade-unions in securing passage
of the Factory Acts. But they fail to consider the question
raised by their example. How is political activity of this sort
connected with development of *socialist* class-consciousness
or a *socialist* political party?

Surveying the situation nearly twenty years later, Marx
asserted that the trade-union movement, confining itself too
exclusively to the economic struggle, was not yet fully conscious of its power to attack the entire system of wage labour.
But, he continues in the resolution written for the Geneva
Congress of the International, the unions are now awakening
to an understanding of their historical mission. As evidence
he cites participation of English trade unions in the movement to extend the suffrage. Yet once again he fails to consider the question raised by his example. How is a struggle
to win workers the vote in a capitalist state connected with
development of *socialist* class-consciousness or a *socialist* political party?

When the International was established in 1864, this
doctrine of the connection between economic and political
struggle was neither explicitly accepted nor explicitly reject-

ed. In the *Inaugural Address* Marx states that conquest of political power has become the great duty of the working class. And in the *General Rules* he states that economic emancipation of the working class is the end to which every political movement ought to be subordinated as a means. But because this issue deeply divided the membership, little attempt was made to connect these statements or to draw the tactical conclusions they implied. During the first six years of its existence, the activities of the International were primarily concerned with economic struggles.

With Marx's defense of the Paris Commune in 1871, the International sharply shifted its attention from problems of trade-union cooperation to problems of proletarian revolution. And in that year the London Conference passed a resolution, written in part by Marx, which explicitly adopted his doctrine of political action. This resolution can be summarized in two theses. First, the proletariat can act as a class only by constituting itself a distinct political party, opposed to all parties formed by the possessing classes. And second, conquest of political power by the proletariat is a necessary condition for triumph of the social revolution.

Behind these general principles lay a definite tactical plan. As interpreted by Marx, the first principle asserts that a socialist party should compete with other parties within the legal framework of the capitalist state—specifically, that it should participate in elections. The second principle, according to his interpretation, asserts that winning elections is a preparation—not a substitute—for revolutionary conquest of political power. This doctrine of political action stresses both the opportunities and the limitations of capitalist democracy.

4

In 1867 the bulk of the urban working class acquired
the vote in England. Three years later the French established
their Third Republic on the basis of universal manhood suffrage. Bismarck incorporated the same principle in the German Empire he created during the following year. After
1871, the connection between socialist tactics and capitalist
democracy became a major preoccupation of Marxian
theory.

Universal suffrage is not mentioned in the *Communist
Manifesto*. But in other writings of the same period Marx
analyzed the consequences of appealing to this principle
under the concrete conditions prevailing in specific countries. The case of France in 1848 is discussed in his *Class
Struggles in France*. The case of Germany in 1850 is discussed in the *First Address to the Communist League*. He
concluded, as I have pointed out in describing the pattern
of permanent revolution, that during the period from 1848
through 1850 a proletarian revolution in France or Germany
could gain majority support only *after* the seizure of power.

Under the conditions prevailing in France a generation
later, Marx believed, universal suffrage had acquired a different significance for the socialist movement. In 1880 he
dictated to Guesde the general portion of a program for the
French socialist party. The program states that socialism can
result only from the revolutionary activity of the proletariat,
organized into a distinct political party. It then adds that
"such an organization must be sought for by all means
available to the proletariat, including universal suffrage, which

can be transformed from an instrument of deception—as up to now it has been—into an instrument of emancipation."

This new approach to universal suffrage was implicit in the advice that Marx and Engels had given German socialists during the years since the establishment of Bismarck's Empire. Engels, in his *Introduction to Marx's 'Class Struggles in France'*, connects the statement in the French program with the achievements of the German party. German socialists, he claims, supplied socialists of all countries with a new weapon, and one of the sharpest, in demonstrating the proper use of universal suffrage.

Universal suffrage is transformed into an instrument of emancipation to the extent that it is used to organize and educate the working class. This claim distinguishes Marx's position from the anarchist contention that workers should not participate in bourgeois elections. But universal suffrage remains an instrument of deception to the extent that it fosters the delusion that to win elections is to win state power. This claim distinguishes Marx's position from that of the vulgar democrats. A vulgar democrat, according to the *Critique of the Gotha Program*, "sees the millenium in the democratic republic and has no suspicion that the class struggle must be fought out to a conclusion precisely within this final form of the state in capitalist society."

Marx presents two major arguments for his contention that electoral struggle is a preparation, not a substitute, for revolution. The first applies to capitalist states with highly developed and relatively autonomous bureaucracies, military and civilian. The second applies to all capitalist states, with or without such bureaucracies.

In the seventies of the nineteenth century France and

Germany were states with highly developed and relatively autonomous bureaucracies. In such states, Marx argued, if a socialist party were voted into office, the bureaucracy— military and civilian—would revolt against the verdict of universal suffrage. Electoral victory would be the prelude to civil war. Marx and Engels, in their 1872 Preface to the *Communist Manifesto,* point to the experience of the Paris Commune as showing that the working class cannot simply take over and use for its own purposes the existing state machinery. The right to govern may be won by the socialist movement peacefully, through electoral victories. But the power to govern can be won only forcibly, by smashing the resistance of the military-bureaucratic state machine.

In the seventies of the nineteenth century England and the United States, in Marx's opinion, lacked highly developed and relatively autonomous bureaucracies. Yet though it might be easier in such states for a socialist party to take over the government, what would happen when this new government attempted to use its power for the radical transformation of society? Commenting in 1878 concerning the Reichstag debate on a proposal to outlaw the Social Democratic Party for advocating force and violence, Marx wrote: "If, for example, in England or the United States the working class were to win a majority in Parliament or Congress, it could legally put an end to laws and institutions standing in the way of its development. . . . Nevertheless, the 'peaceful' movement could be turned into a 'violent' one by revolt of those whose interests were bound up with the old order. If they were crushed by force (as in the American Civil War and the French Revolution), it would be as rebels against the 'lawful' power." Engels testifies, in his 1886 Preface to

Capital, that even for England Marx considered such a "pro-slavery rebellion" not only possible but probable.

5

Taken in their interconnection as a model of the transition from capitalism to socialism, the six principles constituting the pattern of increasing misery point to a majority revolution. The transition will be revolutionary, rather than peaceful, to the extent that mutiny of bureaucrats and rebellion of exploiters lead from electoral and trade-union struggle to civil war. But this transition will be the work of the majority to the extent that class polarization transforms a majority of the population into wage-workers, increasing misery causes them to reject the existing order, and their experience in electoral and trade-union struggles provides them with the organization and knowledge required for carrying out a socialist revolution.

The shift of emphasis in Marx's tactical writings, from the pattern of permanent revolution in the years from 1844 through 1850 to the pattern of increasing misery in the years from 1864 to 1883, is a shift from problems of minority revolution to problems of majority revolution. At no point in his later writings did Marx explicitly contrast the two patterns, presenting his reasons for moving from one set of assumptions to the other. Tensions between his earlier and later doctrines were obscured rather than resolved. His clearest presentations of the tactics of permanent revolution— *The Class Struggles in France* and *The First Address to the*

Communist League—were not republished during his life-time. The *Communist Manifesto* was often republished. But as my discussion of the two patterns has shown, that document can be read both ways.

The task of openly rejecting the pattern of permanent revolution fell to Engels, who did not complete it until twelve years after Marx's death. Appropriately, the occasion for an explicit repudiation was publication of a second edition of *The Class Struggles in France.* Yet the critique of minority revolution which Engels presented in his *Introduction* of 1895 had behind it a history of more than twenty years. It can be regarded as the final attempt of the surviving partner to deal with the problems raised for Marx and Engels by their defense of the Paris Commune.

In the *Second Address of the International Working-men's Association on the Franco-Prussian War,* which Marx wrote after the defeat at Sedan and the proclamation of the Third Republic, he warned the French working class that any attempt to overthrow the new government under the guns of the German army would be an act of desperate folly. When the Commune was established six months later, not one of its leaders considered himself a follower of Marx. The majority were followers of Blanqui and not even members of the International, which they considered a reformist rather than a revolutionary organization. The minority were members of the International, but disciples of Proudhon rather than of Marx. Marx's address to the International, *The Civil War in France,* is an affirmation of solidarity with the defeated revolutionaries rather than a critical estimate of the programs they offered and the tactics they pursued. Ten years later, in a private letter to Domela-Niewenhuis, he asserted, first, that the Commune was no more than the rising of a single city under exceptional circumstances, and second, that its majority were in no sense socialists. With a small amount of common sense, he adds, the Communards could have reached a compromise with Versailles useful to the whole mass of the people—the only goal attainable under the conditions of that time.

Yet when all these qualifications are taken into account, the decisive fact remains that Marx identified the International as an organization and himself as a political leader with the cause of the Commune. On the one hand, this action alarmed and alienated the representatives of British trade-unionism, who of all groups in the International had most consistently supported Marx in the past. It seems probable that the International would have broken up in any case, even if there had been no Commune or if Marx had remained silent after its defeat. But certainly the impact of the Commune was a major factor in accelerating and dramatizing the process of disintegration. On the other hand, Marx's action had an opposite effect upon his recognition as a political leader. The *Civil War in France* transformed him from a relatively obscure theorist into the most famous representative of revolutionary socialism. During 1848 the bourgeoisie had attached the name of Blanqui to the spectre that was haunting Europe. After 1871 that spectre was rechristened with the name of Marx.

Marx's defense of the Commune brought him closer to the followers of Blanqui than he had been at any time since 1850. But this second alliance fell apart over the same issue that had broken up the first: the Blanquists refused to recognize that the revolutionary crisis had ended. In 1874

Engels attacked their conspiratorial romanticism in *The Program of the Blanquist Communards in Exile*. His characterization of Blanqui in this essay differs significantly from that presented by Marx more than twenty years earlier in *The Class Struggles in France*. Engels attacks Blanqui as a proponent of minority revolution.

The tactics of Blanqui, according to Engels, are based on the assumption that a small, highly organized minority, seizing the opportune moment for a revolutionary attempt, can gain some initial successes, carry the mass of the people with them, and successfully complete the revolution. "Blanqui's assumption that a revolution can be made by insurrection of a small minority," he continues, "entails the necessity for a dictatorship after the success of the uprising. This is, of course, not a dictatorship of the proletariat, of the entire revolutionary class. It is instead a dictatorship of the small minority who have made the revolution, and who are themselves organized under the dictatorship of one or several individuals." Blanqui, concludes Engels (his gift for prophecy deserting him), is a revolutionary of the preceding generation.

Two questions are raised by this characterization. First, how accurately does it describe the tactics of Blanqui? And second, to what extent does it apply to the tactics advocated by Marx and Engels when they too were revolutionaries of the preceding generation?

To support his thesis, Engels points to Blanqui's leadership of the insurrection attempted by the Society of the Seasons in 1839. Yet he makes no effort to analyze the far more complicated tactics advocated by Blanqui during 1848 and at later periods. It could be argued that while Marx in 1850 exaggerated the similarity between his principles and those of Blanqui, Engels in 1874 exaggerated the contrast.

In this essay Engels criticized Blanqui without discussing the extent to which at one time he and Marx had advocated similar tactics. But twenty years later, in his *Introduction to Marx's 'Class Struggles in France'*, he took this second step. Here criticism has become self-criticism. Engels attacks as incorrect, even for that time, the tactics he and Marx had advocated in the period from 1844 through 1850. His basic argument is that such tactics represent a program of minority revolution.

6

In 1895, when Engels wrote his *Introduction,* leaders of the German Social Democrats feared passage of a new law suppressing their party for advocating violent overthrow of the government. Under their pressure, he deleted from his manuscript all passages explicitly considering the prospect of armed conflict with the existing government. After Engels died, Bernstein argued from the published text that the *Introduction* was a formal renunciation of revolutionary tactics. After the Russian Revolution, Leninists argued from the restored text that this was not the case. Yet, by ignoring the contrast between minority and majority revolution, both arguments oversimplify Engels' actual position. The restored deletions show that he rejects the tactics of peace and legality at any price. His main argument explicitly rejects the tactics of minority revolution. The tactics he advocates are those of majority revolution.

In the period of 1848, according to the *Introduction,*
Marx and Engels based their theory of revolution mainly
upon the historical experience of France from 1789 to 1830.
They believed that 1848 was another 1789—the start of a
long, tumultuous revolutionary period, which in this case
would end with victory for the proletariat. But history, writes
Engels with the hindsight of nearly half a century, has
proved them wrong in two respects. First, it has revealed the
error of their theories. Second, it has wholly transformed the
conditions under which the proletariat has to fight. For
both reasons, the tactics of 1848 are inappropriate for the
conditions of 1895.

The crucial point, according to the *Introduction,* is that
in 1848 Marx and Engels thought in terms of minority
revolution. In every bourgeois revolution the majority had
either remained passive and neutral or had actively supported
decisions made by a minority. Revolutionary struggle decided which minority the majority accepted or supported;
and the outcome was transfer of political rule from one
minority to another. During the years of revolutionary crisis
from 1848 through 1850, Marx and Engels expected the
proletarian revolution to follow the same pattern. "Was not
this a situation where a revolution could succeed, led indeed
by a minority, but this time in the majority's own interest?"
Later, to the extent that experience educated the majority
to understand their interests, minority revolution would become majority revolution.

"History," comments Engels, "has proved us, and all
who thought like us, wrong." In the first place, the economic
revolution which spread over all of Continental Europe
during the decades after 1848 has shown that economic con-

ditions were not, by a long way, ripe for putting an end to capitalist production. In the second place, the experience of the Commune has shown that, twenty years after 1848, rule by the working class was still impossible. On the one hand, the rest of France left Paris in the lurch. On the other hand, the strength of the Commune was dissipated in aimless quarrels between the Blanquist majority and the Proudhonist minority, neither of whom knew what to do. The workers' government in 1871 proved no more fruitful than their surprise attack in 1848.

Nevertheless, Engels argues, the same economic development that has proved incorrect the tactics of 1848 has provided the basis for a different pattern of transition. In the first place, it has greatly accelerated the polarization of European society into an industrial bourgeoisie and an industrial proletariat. In the second place, it has greatly increased the intensity of the struggle between these classes. Furthermore, the European proletariat has become organized into a great international army of socialists, educated by Marxian theory to a clear understanding of its task. "If even this mighty proletarian army has not yet reached its goal, and if, far from winning victory with one great blow, it must slowly advance from one position to another in hard, tenacious struggle, this proves beyond any doubt how impossible it was in 1848 to reorganize society by means of a simple surprise attack."

Engels' *Introduction* does not renounce all revolutionary tactics. But it explicitly repudiates the pattern of permanent revolution which he and Marx had developed many years before, inspired by the tradition of Babeuf, Buonarroti, and Blanqui.

7

On another issue, of at least equal importance, Marx's pattern of increasing misery is in agreement with the tactical doctrines of Blanqui. The pattern of increasing misery—no less than the pattern of permanent revolution—embodies the central principle of revolutionary socialism, the thesis that seizure of state power by the proletariat must precede any socialist transformation of the economy. This principle, sometimes formulated as the thesis that the political revolution must precede the social revolution, is challenged both by reformist socialists and by anarchists, though for different reasons. Anarchists identify social revolution with the abolition of political rule. They argue that the task of the workers is simply to destroy the capitalist state, not to replace it with a state of their own. Reformists deny that social transformation must wait for political revolution. They argue that the task of the workers is to promote piecemeal transformation of capitalist institutions into socialist institutions, not to postpone the introduction of socialism until after a revolutionary seizure of power. Conflict among representatives of these three positions was a major factor in destroying the First International. At the decisive Hague Congress in 1872 the majority, consisting of Marxists and Blanquists, defended the thesis that the political revolution must precede the social revolution. They were opposed, on the one hand, by anarchist followers of Bakunin and, on the other hand, by reformists from the British trade-unions.

The conflict between Marxism and anarchism reached its height in 1872, when the International supported Marx's position on political action. During the succeeding year Marx, in his essay *Politische Indifferentismus,* attacked the anarchist rejection of any political or economic struggle for reforms before the revolution. Engels, in a companion essay *On Authority,* attacked their rejection of any political or economic authority after the revolution. Both essays touch upon, but do not stress, an important consequence of the Marxian position. If the political revolution must precede the social revolution, then even a majority revolution may require a period of proletarian dictatorship.

During the same year in which these essays were written Bakunin, in his *Statehood and Anarchy,* attacked the Marxian doctrine of proletarian dictatorship. When the proletariat becomes the ruling class, he asks, over whom will it rule? Marx, in his notes on Bakunin's book, replies that when the proletariat wins state power the old organization of society has not yet disappeared. The proletariat must use political coercion to continue its class struggle against the capitalists, until the economic conditions which give rise to classes have been abolished or transformed. The dictatorship of the proletariat, though transitional, will not be brief. It will last as long as this process of social transformation.

The contrast between Marxism and reformism is less clearly defined. According to Marx's formula in the French program of 1880, socialism can result only from the revolutionary activity of the proletariat, organized into a distinct political party. But how is this statement to be interpreted? Does it mean that there can be no socialism at all until after the proletariat seizes power? Or does it mean that transformation of capitalist into socialist institutions can be *completed* only in this fashion? In Marx's model of the transition from feudalism to capitalism, bourgeois revolution comes at the

end of a long period during which the economy of capitalism
has successfully competed with the economy of feudalism.
There political revolution is not the commencement, but the
completion, of social revolution. Why should the transition
from capitalism to socialism follow a different pattern?

In his *Inaugural Address* of 1864 Marx cites two instances of socialist institutions developing inside capitalist
society: the cooperative movement and factory legislation.
Cooperatives have demonstrated in practice the feasibility of
large-scale production without capitalists. Enactment of the
Ten Hours' Bill was the first victory of the political economy
of the proletariat, social production controlled by social foresight, over the political economy of the bourgeoisie, blind
rule of supply and demand. This discussion points toward a
model of the transition from capitalism to socialism—distinct from both the pattern of permanent revolution and the
pattern of increasing misery—which I have nicknamed the
pattern of competing systems.

To develop the suggestions of Marx's *Inaugural Address*
into a pattern for the transition from capitalism to socialism
is to challenge some of the central claims embodied in the
pattern of increasing misery. What can the proletariat achieve
by struggling for reforms within capitalist society? According
to the pattern of increasing misery, economic and political
struggles serve the cause of socialism *solely* by organizing and
educating the working class. This is equivalent to the claim
that the social revolution cannot start until the political
revolution has triumphed. But suppose this claim is ques-
tioned. Then economic and political struggles can be viewed
in a very different light, as steps in a lengthy, gradual process of transforming capitalist institutions into socialist in-

stitutions. Whether this process of social transformation will
eventually lead to political revolution is not the point at issue.
The question is whether, without a political revolution, the
social transformation can begin.

After Engels' death the polemics of Kautsky and Bernstein marked the transformation of this latent tension in
Marx's thought into an open conflict of divergent political tendencies. Kautsky and the orthodox Marxists defended the pattern of increasing misery. Bernstein and the
revisionists proposed to alter Marxian theory to the extent
required for replacing the pattern of increasing misery with
the pattern of competing systems. Bernstein's first revisionist
essay, *Utopismus und Eklekticismus,* was a rejection of
"catastrophism," an attack on the thesis that socialist transformation must wait for political revolution.

8

Of all doctrines relating the struggle for reforms to
the attainment of socialism, by far the hardest to apply in
practice is the doctrine that such struggle is indispensable
yet serves the cause of socialism solely by organizing and
educating the working class. It is easy to formulate a program based on the doctrine that any struggle for reform
serves simply to divert the proletariat from its major task,
the revolutionary overthrow of capitalism. It is not hard to
formulate a program based on the doctrine that economic
and political reforms can promote piecemeal transformation
of capitalism into socialism. But the attempt to find a path

between these positions quite regularly results in sharp disputes when Marxian socialists seek to formulate their program and tactics with respect to specific issues.

Those who stress the task of organizing the working class are likely to concentrate on activating the maximum number. This may incline them to put forward attainable demands and to emphasize immediate advantages. The danger of this policy is that such tactics may result in blunting rather than sharpening the revolutionary consciousness of the workers. On the other hand, those who stress the task of educating the working class are likely to concentrate on turning the maximum number into revolutionaries. This may incline them to put forward unattainable demands and to ignore immediate advantages. The danger of this policy is that such tactics may result in isolating the revolutionary socialists from the less class-conscious workers. These two ways of falling off the tightrope—sacrificing revolutionary fervour to numbers and sacrificing numbers to revolutionary fervour—are forms of what came to be known, in the era after Marx, as right and left deviations.

To the extent that these conflicting tendencies are justified in terms of theory, they may become associated with different patterns for the transition from capitalism to socialism. According to the pattern of increasing misery, the tasks of the socialist movement are to win a majority, to seize power, and to transform society—in that order of priority. A persistent tendency to place more emphasis upon revolutionary consciousness than upon numerical support may lead to a different order of priorities: first seizure of power, then transformation of society, and finally winning a majority. That is the order embodied in the pattern of permanent revolution.

A persistent tendency to place more emphasis upon numerical support than upon revolutionary consciousness may lead to still another order of priorities: first transformation of society, then winning a majority, then seizure of power. That is the order embodied in the pattern of competing systems. Conflict among advocates of these three tactics provides a theoretical dimension for the internal politics of Marxian socialism.

Engels died in 1895. At that time the pattern of increasing misery was almost universally accepted by socialists calling themselves followers of Marx. But in 1896 the first essay of Bernstein's *Probleme des Socialismus* appeared, and in 1899 his *Evolutionary Socialism*. In 1902 Lenin published *What is to be Done?* and in 1905 *Two Tactics*. Ten years after the death of Engels the monopoly of one pattern had given way to the hotly disputed contest of all three.

Stalin died in 1953. By that time most Social Democrats no longer professed themselves followers of Marx. The pattern of minority revolution elaborated by Lenin, modified by the doctrine of socialism in one country and the doctrine of forced collectivization of agriculture, was almost universally accepted by socialists calling themselves followers of Marx. But in 1958 appeared the new Program of the Communist League of Yugoslavia, adopting and elaborating the pattern of competing systems. Then in 1960 appeared the *Statement of Eighty-One Communist Parties*. Side by side in that declaration, set forth almost in alternate paragraphs, can be discerned the Chinese reaffirmation of Leninist orthodoxy and the Russian attempt to revive the pattern of majority revolution. The conflict of three tactics, which once split the Social Democrats, now splits the Communists in turn.

MARX
AND
REFORMISM

1

In the transition from feudalism to capitalism, according to the Marxian model of that process, the capitalist class conquers political power at the end of a long period during which the economy of capitalism has successfully competed with the economy of feudalism. Arguing in *Anti-Dühring* against theories asserting the primacy of politics over economics, Engels describes the growth and triumph of capitalism in the following terms: "Originally an oppressed estate, paying tribute to the feudal nobility, recruited from serfs and vassals of all sorts, the burghers conquered one strong point after another in constant struggle with the nobility, and finally in the most developed countries took their place as rulers—in France by directly overthrowing them, in England by making them increasingly bourgeois and annexing them as ornamental heads of the capitalist class. How was this accomplished? Entirely through change in the 'economic situation', which was followed sooner or later, voluntarily or as the result of struggle, by a change in political conditions. The struggle of the bourgeoisie against the feudal nobility was the struggle of city against countryside, industry against landed property, money economy against natural economy; and the decisive weapon of the burghers in this struggle was their *economic* power position, constantly strengthened through the development of handicraft industry, later of manufacturing industry, and through the extension of trade."

The transition from feudalism to capitalism is similarly described in *Capital* and in the *Communist Manifesto*. From the start of the sixteenth century, according to Marx, capitalist economic institutions oppose, permeate, and replace feudal economic institutions. When the capitalists seize political power, after 1640 in England and after 1789 in France, society has already been decisively transformed.

Could the transition from capitalism to socialism follow a similar pattern? Jaurès, in his essay *The Question of Method,* argues that it must. "History shows many instances of the coexistence of different and even contradictory forms. For example, guild production and capitalist production functioned side by side throughout the seventeenth and eighteenth centuries. Free agricultural labour and serfdom also coexisted for a long time. I am convinced that in the revolutionary evolution that will lead us to communism we shall have throughout a long period the juxtaposition of collectivist property and private property, of communism and capitalism. This is indeed the law of such great transformations."

Arguing from this standpoint, Jaurès explicitly rejects both the Marxian pattern of permanent revolution and the Marxian pattern of increasing misery. The principle of competing systems, which he presents as a law of history, is the theoretical starting point of reformist socialism.

2

Instead of a single model of the transition from capitalism to socialism, the tradition of competing systems presents a large family of models, with a corresponding array of programs and tactical doctrines. Among the predecessors of Marx some major theorists representing this tradition are

Fourier and Owen; among Marx's contemporaries, Blanc, Mill, and Lassalle; and in the succeeding generation, Sidney Webb, Tugan-Baranowski, Bernstein, and Jaurès. Rather than attempt to discuss them all, I shall select for examination three British reformists: Owen, Mill, and Webb.

For a brief period in his career Owen proposed to introduce socialism at one stroke through refusal of the workers, united in trade unions, to continue capitalist production. But the pattern he advocated for many years, both before and after this point, was one of gradual and piecemeal transition. According to this program, the first step is to establish a number of cooperative villages, each of from five hundred to two thousand members. The economy of each village will be both agricultural and industrial, so that each can achieve a large measure of self-sufficiency. Members of such cooperatives will be recruited initially from the unemployed. Funds, Owen suggests in his *Six Lectures Delivered in Manchester,* could be provided from four sources. The most desirable method of establishing such villages would be for the existing governments of Europe and America to finance them. If the national governments prove unwilling to act, local authorities could act in their place. If the local authorities also prove unwilling, "the more enlightened and benevolent members of all classes may unite in joint-stock companies to carry these measures into full execution . . ." And if the upper and middle classes hold back, funds could be raised through weekly subscriptions from members of the working classes.

Once the first cooperatives have been established to provide for the unemployed, these pilot projects will demonstrate the overwhelming superiority of socialism over capitalism.

The force of example will then do the rest. Proposing in his *Lectures* that existing governments provide the funds, Owen prophesies the outcome: "In this manner governments would commence their improvements with the lowest and most miserable class in their states, and would gradually improve upwards, until all the members of these governments would themselves desire to be translated into the new world, that they might also enjoy the superior state of existence. . . . By this mode of introducing change, disorder would be avoided, and every injury to any class or any individual, be prevented." As the cooperative sector continues to grow and the capitalist sector continues to shrink, the socialist era will arrive like a thief in the night.

John Stuart Mill presents a more complex and qualified version of the same general pattern. In his *Principles of Political Economy* he argues that cooperatives which distribute income according to contribution will prove more practicable, at least in the immediate future, than those which distribute income in equal shares. He does not envisage government aid as a means for establishing such associations. Instead, he believes that they will be created indirectly, by transformation of capitalist enterprises through profit-sharing, or directly, on the initiative of the workers themselves.

As cooperatives increase in numbers and demonstrate their advantages in practice, Mill predicts, the abler workers will no longer consent to spend their lives as wage-earners. "As associations multiplied," he writes in the chapter of his *Principles* dealing with the future of the labouring classes, "they would tend more and more to absorb all work-people, except those who have too little understanding, or too little virtue, to be capable of learning to act on any other system than that of narrow selfishness. As this change proceeded, owners of capital would gradually find it to their advantage, instead of maintaining the struggle of the old system with work-people of only the worst description, to lend their capital to the associations; to do this at a diminishing rate of interest, and at last, perhaps, even to exchange their capital for terminable annuities. In this or some such mode, the existing accumulations of capital might honestly, and by a kind of spontaneous process, become in the end the joint property of all who participate in their productive employment: a transformation which, thus effected, . . . would be the nearest approach to social justice, and the most beneficial ordering of industrial affairs for the universal good, which it is possible at present to foresee.''

Mill differs from Owen in denying that all advantages are on the side of socialism. In the ability of its managers and in its readiness to innovate, he believes, a socialist association is likely to prove inferior to a capitalist enterprise. Furthermore, he argues that socialist writers have exaggerated the evils of capitalism and underestimated the possibilities of reform within the existing system. Competition breeds selfishness, as socialists like Owen claim. But it also stimulates effort and promotes efficiency, so that competition—at least between cooperative associations—would be highly desirable for a socialist society. Private property has resulted in social inequality. But, Mill argues in the chapter of his *Principles* on property, if legislation were directed toward diffusing—instead of concentrating—wealth, the principle of individual property would be found to have no necessary connection with the physical and social evils which almost all socialist writers assume to be inseparable from it.

During the period of competing systems, Mill believed, the capitalist system could be controlled or reformed through legislative action, in such fashion as to smooth out the process of transition. By 1869, when he wrote his unfinished *Chapters on Socialism,* a large proportion of the urban wage-workers in England had won the right to vote. In the first of these essays he remarks that, though the working classes have not yet used their recently acquired electoral power to promote their collective interests, they will certainly take such action before long. "And when they do so," he adds, "it will not be in the disorderly and ineffective way which belongs to a people not habituated to the use of legal and constitutional machinery, nor will it be by the impulse of a mere instinct of levelling. The instruments will be the press, public meetings and associations, and the return to Parliament of the greatest possible number of persons pledged to the political aims of the working classes."

Socialists like Owen and Mill speculated about a gradual and peaceful replacement of capitalism by socialism: Sidney Webb announced—in 1889—that this transition had been under way for half a century. In his contribution to the *Fabian Essays* he describes socialism as the extension of democratic principles to economic organization. In the shift from economic individualism to economic collectivism, resulting from the growth of political democracy, four main currents can be discerned. First, there has been a replacement of private enterprise by public ownership, municipal or national. Second, there has been an increase in public regulation of those parts of the economy still under private control. Third, there has been a rise in public appropriation of unearned incomes, through taxes on rent and profit.

Fourth, there has been an expansion in the use of public funds for the welfare of the poorer sections of the community. Comparing the unfettered capitalism that characterized the beginning of the nineteenth century with the economic organization at its close, Webb writes: "So little element of permanence was there in this individualistic order that, with the progress of political emancipation, private ownership of the means of production has been, in one direction or another, successively regulated, limited and superseded, until it may now fairly be claimed that the socialist philosophy of today is but the conscious and explicit assertion of principles of social organization which have been already in great part unconsciously adopted. The economic history of the century is an almost continuous record of the progress of socialism."

Webb describes this process as unconscious, stressing the extent to which it has been unplanned and even unforeseen. Its ultimate cause, he asserts, has been the pressure of technology upon institutions. The Industrial Revolution has concentrated the producers in factories, the population in cities. These economic changes have resulted in the development of democratic political institutions. The inevitable outcome of industrialization and democracy is socialism.

Even though losers as well as gainers become increasingly aware of what is happening, can this radical transformation of society be carried to completion through gradual, piecemeal, peaceful changes? Will the receivers of rent and profit submit without a struggle? In his contribution to the *Fabian Essays* Webb asserts that, in England at least, capitalism can be abolished wholly through constitutional and peaceful changes. Within the limits of that essay he does not commit himself concerning other countries. In his *Socialism in England,* which was published in the same year as the *Fabian Essays,* he explicitly refuses to provide a general formula. There is, he argues, no universally applicable socialist method of reform. He denies that the transition to socialism must necessarily, or even normally, involve a sudden and forcible overthrow of the existing government. But he suggests that it cannot be peaceful in every case. Contrasting the obstacles confronting socialists in Russia with the greater political freedom prevailing in Germany and France, he concludes that the tactics of a socialist movement must depend primarily upon the nature of the repressive forces it encounters.

3

The revisionist movement was born in 1896 when Bernstein, influenced by the Fabians, undertook to revise Marxian theory and tactics along reformist lines. Since that time the term "revisionist" has been given an increasingly wider application. For example, the Program adopted in 1958 by the Communist League of Yugoslavia describes as revisionist the "statist-pragmatic" modifications of Marxian theory introduced by Stalin. Yet the word becomes so vague as to be quite useless if it is stretched to cover *any* attempt to alter Marxian theory. I propose to restrict its reference to attempts, starting within the Marxian movement, to alter both theory and tactics along reformist lines. As I use the term, all revisionists are reformists. Bernstein, for example, is both. But not all reformists are revisionists. Webb and Jaurès, for example, are not revisionists, though their theoretical and tactical doctrines are quite similar to those of Bernstein.

In *Evolutionary Socialism* Bernstein opens his critique of Marxism by arguing that the tactics of permanent revolution are incompatible with the outlook of historical materialism. Far from being based on careful analysis of political and economic conditions, the tactical doctrines set forth by Marx and Engels in 1848 were based on not much more than speculative fantasy—a chance conjunction between the Hegelian mystique of contradiction and the Blanquist mystique of insurrection. Unrealistic even for that era, these doctrines have proved wholly irrelevant to the conditions confronted by the socialist movement in later generations.

Engels' repudiation of the pattern of permanent revolution in his *Introduction to Marx's 'Class Struggles in France'* Bernstein describes as a political testament. But the bulk of Bernstein's book is devoted to attacking the pattern of increasing misery, which Engels' "testament" had accepted as the alternative basis for socialist tactics. The theses of class polarization and increasing misery have not been confirmed by the facts of capitalist development; a tactical program based upon such predictions is permanently divorced from reality. Why then did Engels refuse to face the facts? Because, though he took a step forward in abandoning the Blanquist tactics of permanent revolution, he failed to complete his emancipation. The pattern of increasing misery, no less than the pattern of permanent revolution, embodies the Blanquist dogma that conquest of political power through proletarian revolution must precede any socialist transformation of the economy.

The key to Bernstein's critique of Marxism is his proposal to replace both the pattern of permanent revolution and
the pattern of increasing misery with a pattern of competing
systems. In an essay on the theory of capitalist breakdown—
subsequently collected in his *Probleme des Socialismus*—he
wrote, from the standpoint of 1898: "It is my firm convic-
tion that the present generation will see the realization of a
great deal of socialism, if not in the patented form then at
least in substance. The steady expansion of the obligations of
society to individuals and of the duties and corresponding
rights of individuals with respect to society; the extension of
the right of supervision over economic life exercised by society organized as nation or as state; the development of
democratic self-government in municipality, county, and
province; and the enlargement of the tasks of these bodies—
all these signify for me growth into socialism or, if you will,
piecemeal realization of socialism. The transfer of economic
enterprises from private to public management will of course
accompany this development, but it will proceed only
gradually."

4

Does this position amount to a revision of Marxism, as
Bernstein claimed? Or is it nothing less than an abandonment
of Marxism, as Bernstein's orthodox opponents claimed? The
first step in answering this question is to state the major issues
involved. One is the claim that socialist transformation of a
capitalist economy can *start* without a political revolution.

Another is the claim that socialist transformation of a capitalist economy can *finish* without a political revolution. Bernstein seems to have affirmed both the starting and the finishing theses: Kautsky seems to have denied both. Yet their failure to analyze these issues separately was a source of confusion on both sides.

The orthodox definition of reformism was formulated by Kautsky in his *Social Reform and Revolution*—and endorsed by Lenin in his *Platform of Revolutionary Social Democracy*. According to this definition, reformist socialists are socialists who propose to transform capitalist society into socialist society *solely* through reforms. Kautsky writes: "Those who repudiate on principle political revolution as a means of social transformation, who seek to confine this transformation to such measures as can be obtained from the ruling classes, are *social reformers*—no matter how opposed their ideal may be to the existing form of society. . . . Not striving for social reforms, but explicitly limiting oneself to them, is what distinguishes a social reformer from a social revolutionary." A theorist who holds that socialist transformation of a capitalist economy can start, but cannot finish, without a political revolution is not a reformist in the sense defined.

Yet Kautsky does not restrict his argument to reformists in the sense defined. Both in *Social Reform and Revolution* and in *The Road to Power* his discussion lumps together the thesis that socialist transformation cannot finish without political revolution and the thesis that it cannot start without political revolution. At the end of the first chapter of *The Road to Power,* for example, he explicitly includes in his attack those socialists who do not doubt that a revolution will come but believe it to be at least one generation away.

Bernstein, on the other hand, dismisses as caricature the accusation that he proposes to restrict social transformation to such reforms as can be obtained from the ruling classes. No one denies, he writes in his Preface to *Evolutionary Socialism,* the necessity for the working classes to gain control of the government. What is denied is that all measures of socialist transformation must be postponed until after that event. The issue is not finishing but starting.

Yet Bernstein does not restrict himself to arguing that socialist transformation can start without political revolution. At some points in *Evolutionary Socialism* he asserts that for a long time yet the working class cannot conquer political power and concludes that during this time the socialist movement should concentrate on struggling for piecemeal reforms. But at other points he asserts that development of democratic institutions diminishes the probability of a revolution at *any* stage, however remote, in the process of socialist transformation. Kautsky, in failing to separate the two questions, followed the precedent set by his opponent.

The specific tactical questions most hotly disputed by reformist and revolutionary socialists in England, France, and Germany at the turn of the century—whether to form electoral alliances, whether to participate in coalition governments, what attitude to take toward nationalization measures or welfare legislation while the government is still in capitalist hands—pose problems of starting rather than of finishing. Suppose a theorist takes the position that political revolution, though unavoidable, will come at a point when socialist transformation of the economy is already well advanced. He is likely then to argue that the most important factor in organizing and educating the great majority who stand to gain from socialism will be their actual experience of benefits achieved through piecemeal reforms. When confronted with a tactical decision—whether to form an electoral alliance, whether to enter a coalition government, whether to support a specific nationalization measure, or whether to vote for specific welfare legislation—the first question such a theorist asks is what policy is most likely to advance the gradual, cumulative process of reform. At some point in this process, he predicts, conflicts of interest between those who lose and those who gain will explode into civil war. But before that point is reached, he contends, only a partial attainment of socialism can educate and organize an anti-capitalist army strong enough to win.

Consider, by contrast, a theorist who denies that socialist transformation can start without political revolution. He is likely then to argue that reforms, in so far as they are attainable at all under capitalism, should be regarded simply as by-products of revolutionary struggle. What serves the cause of socialism is not attaining a reform but fighting for it. Battles, not palliatives, are what organize and educate the working class. When confronted with a tactical decision— whether to form an electoral alliance, whether to enter a coalition government, whether to support a specific nationalization measure, whether to vote for specific welfare legislation—the first question such a theorist asks is what policy is most likely to bring nearer the revolutionary seizure of power. Judged by this standard, participating in an electoral alliance or a coalition government in a non-revolutionary situation is inadmissible in principle. Nationalization measures and welfare legislation, though indispensable after the revolution for creating a socialist economy, may serve before the revolution to increase the power of the capitalist state.

These considerations indicate that before the First World War the starting thesis was central for the conflict between reformist and revolutionary socialism. Yet even at that time neither side consistently separated the two issues. And after the First World War changing attitudes toward coalition tactics and nationalization measures shifted the focus of debate from the starting thesis to the finishing thesis. To conform with historical usage, it is advisable to define reformist socialists as those who affirm both theses. But to promote theoretical clarity, it is necessary to analyze separately the arguments for each in turn.

What then is the relation of revisionism to Marxism? If no support can be found in Marx for either thesis, then to advocate revisionist tactics amounts simply to abandoning Marxism for Fabianism. But to the extent that Marx includes among his models of the transition from capitalism to socialism a pattern of competing systems, he provides support for the starting thesis. This question turns primarily upon his analysis of the capitalist economy. And to the extent that he recognizes circumstances under which the transition can be completed without civil war, he provides support for the finishing thesis. This question turns primarily upon his analysis of the capitalist state.

5

Marx's distinction between productive forces and productive relations, as he presents it in the Preface to his

Critique of Political Economy, seems designed to analyze the connection between technology and property. He writes there that the relations between men in the process of social production constitute, as an aggregate, the economic structure of society. Each set of productive relations corresponds to a definite stage in the development of the material forces of production. And each set of such relations is equivalent to a system of property relations: the latter are simply legal expressions of the former.

Taken literally, this account seems grossly to oversimplify the facts. Is not each technique of production a process, involving both forces and relations? Is there anything like a one-to-one correspondence between these relations and property relations? To what extent, for example, do the United States and the Soviet Union share a common technology? To what extent, on the other hand, did English laws of property change during the course of the Industrial Revolution? To describe the connection between technology and property in terms of a contrast between forces and relations seems only a metaphor, and a misleading metaphor at that.

In *Capital* Marx has in effect transformed his contrast between productive forces and relations into a contrast between two kinds of relations, the technologically conditioned and the property conditioned. Discussing, for example, the dual role of management in capitalist production—in his chapter entitled "Cooperation" in the first volume and in his chapter entitled "Interest and Profit of Enterprise" in the third volume—he treats property relations as limited by, but not equivalent to, technological relations. Instead of the technological determinism suggested by some of his early formulations, this approach recognizes an asymmetrical interaction between technology and property. Though Marx continued to attack Mill's contrast between laws of production and laws of distribution, his own contrast between productive forces and productive relations developed definitely in that direction.

To recognize that property relations are limited by, yet not equivalent to, technological relations is to suggest that a society at a given level of technological development may present a variety of coexisting and competing forms of production. The greatest variety and keenest competition might be expected in periods of maximum tension between technology and property. Marx, as I have already pointed out, presents such a pattern in his account of the transition from feudalism to capitalism. In the *Inaugural Address* of the First International and in some chapters of the third volume of *Capital* he indicates, without developing in detail, a similar pattern for the transition from capitalism to socialism.

In two chapters of the third volume of *Capital*—that entitled "Interest and Profit of Enterprise" and that entitled "The Role of Credit in Capitalist Production"—Marx analyzes the significance of the shift from individual capitalist entrepreneurs to joint-stock companies. He asserts there that the development of corporate enterprise radically alters both the character of the ownership of the means of production and the role of the owners in the productive process.

All capitalist production is social, in the sense that each enterprise involves the collective activity of a number of direct producers. Yet normally in capitalist societies the means of production are individually owned. The shift from individual to corporate enterprise alters the opposition between social production and private ownership, because it substitutes collective for individual ownership of the means of production. Corporate capitalist ownership is a transitional form between two extremes: ownership by a single capitalist and ownership by the associated producers. "Within the limits of the capitalist mode of production, it is the transcendence of capital as private property."

The shift from individual to corporate enterprise divorces the owner of the means of production from participation in the process of production. Managerial functions previously performed by individual capitalists are now transferred to salaried administrators. The once indispensable entrepreneur, now shrunk into a rentier, has become as superfluous as the landowner. Corporate capitalist production, managed by salaried administrators for rentier owners, is a transitional form between two extremes: production managed by a single capitalist and production managed by salaried administrators for the associated producers. "Within the capitalist mode of production, this is the transcendence of the capitalist mode of production—a self-annulling contradiction which clearly represents a mere point of transition to a new form of production."

Marx stresses the complexities and conflicts of this development. "It establishes monopolies in certain spheres and thereby provokes the interference of the state. It produces a new financial aristocracy, a new set of parasites in the form of promoters, speculators, and merely nominal directors; and it creates a whole system of swindling and cheating in the fields of speculation, stock issuing, and stock trading. It is private production without the control of private property."

In both chapters of *Capital* where he discusses the shift from individual to corporate enterprise Marx discusses a second transitional form, the cooperative association. To a greater extent than joint-stock companies, cooperatives introduce decisive changes in ownership of the means of production and in management of the productive process. In a cooperative enterprise the dual character of capitalist management disappears, since the manager is paid by the workers instead of representing capital against them. At the same time the opposition between social production and private ownership of the means of production is overcome, though only in the form of the associated workers becoming their own capitalist and using the means of production to realize a profit on their own labour. Cooperative associations represent the development of non-capitalist production within capitalist society. "They show the way in which, at a certain level of development of the material forces of production and of the corresponding social forms of production, a new mode of production grows within and develops out of the old mode of production."

The period during which these different kinds of enterprise—corporate and individual, monopolistic and competitive, cooperative and capitalist—exist side by side presents a complex pattern of competing systems. In the chapters of *Capital* describing this coexistence of the new and the old, Marx affirms the minimum thesis of reformism, that the economic transition from capitalism to socialism can start before the working class attains state power.

6

In the *Inaugural Address* Marx argues that cooperative production cannot replace capitalist production throughout society until after the working class has conquered political power. This amounts to denying that the transition from capitalism to collectivism can be completed solely through economic competition between cooperative and capitalist enterprise. Yet Marx affirms that the transition can start in this fashion. The growth of the cooperative movement within capitalist society represents, he asserts, a major victory for the political economy of labour over the political economy of property.

Marx sees another such victory in the passage of the Factory Acts. In the *Inaugural Address* he claims that enactment of the Ten Hours' Bill marked the first time that in broad daylight the political economy of the bourgeoisie, blind rule of supply and demand, succumbed to the political economy of the proletariat, social production controlled by social foresight. In the field of political control, as in that of economic organization, total victory cannot be obtained until after the working class conquers political power. But in both cases the transition can commence with partial and peaceful changes.

How long can the transition remain peaceful? Granted that at some point the working class must take power, can this change be effected wholly by peaceful means? To ask this question is to shift from the minimum thesis of reformism to its maximum thesis, to the claim that socialist transformation of a capitalist economy can finish without a proletarian revolution. What support can be found in Marx's writings for this second claim?

In a speech delivered to the Amsterdam branch of the First International in 1872, Marx asserts that a peaceful transition to socialism is possible for some countries. After arguing that to establish a socialist society it is necessary for the working class to conquer political power, he adds: "Of course, I must not be understood to imply that the means to this end will be everywhere the same. We know that special regard must be paid to the institutions, customs, and traditions of various lands; and we do not deny that there are certain countries, such as the United States and England, in which the workers may hope to secure their ends by peaceful means. If I am not mistaken, Holland belongs to the same category. Even so, we have to recognize that in most Continental countries force will have to be the lever of the revolution."

What distinguishes countries where peaceful transition is possible from those where it is not? Marx offers a partial answer in a letter he wrote to Kugelmann in April of 1871. There he asserts that for the success of every people's revolution on the Continent it is essential for the revolutionaries, instead of attempting to transfer the military-bureaucratic state machine to their own control, to smash that machine instead. Yet nowhere does he state why this policy is not essential for socialists outside the Continent. Is it because no military-bureaucratic state machine exists in England or the United States? Or is it because the military-bureaucratic machines which do exist in these countries can be transferred to socialist control?

Marx was unquestionably aware of the fact that at the start of the seventies some bureaucratic organization, military and civilian, existed in both England and the United States. Did he base his belief in the possibility of peaceful transition upon the *size* of these bureaucracies? Then if he had lived to observe the subsequent expansion of these military-bureaucratic state machines, he would have abandoned any hope for peaceful transition. This is the interpretation stressed by Lenin in *State and Revolution* and *The Renegade Kautsky.* Or was Marx's belief in the possibility of peaceful transition based on the degree of *control* exercised by elected officials over the bureaucrats of England and the United States, due to the "institutions, customs, and traditions" of these countries? In that case, even though the bureaucracies grew bigger, the possibility of peaceful transition need not be rejected. And to the extent that Continental countries developed similar institutions, customs, and traditions, peaceful transition might become a possibility for them too. This is the interpretation suggested by Engels in his *Critique of a Draft for the Erfurt Program*.

Even for England and the United States, Marx did not rule out the possibility of civil war. He and his party, he wrote to Hyndman in 1880, considered an English revolution "not *necessary*, but—according to historic precedents—*possible*." Suppose the working class could come to power peacefully, without a bureaucratic mutiny. Could the new government then take radical measures for the transformation of society without facing rebellion by the exploiters? On the policy of compensating landlords and capitalists, Engels reports in *The Peasant Question in France and Germany*: "Marx told me (and how often!) that in his opinion we would get off most cheaply if we could buy out the whole lot of them." Lenin interpreted this to mean that in the England of the seventies a policy of compensation might ensure a peaceful transition. In that concrete situation, he writes in *'Left-Wing' Childishness*, "it was perfectly admissible to think of paying the capitalists well, of giving them ransom, *if* the circumstances were such as to impel the capitalists, providing they were bought off, to submit peacefully and to pass over to socialism in a cultured, organized manner." But, according to Engels' account in his Preface to the English translation of *Capital*, Marx was not optimistic.

After reporting that Marx's studies led him to conclude that England was the only country in Europe where the inevitable social revolution might be effected entirely by peaceful and legal means, Engels remarks: "He certainly never forgot to add that he hardly expected the English ruling classes to submit, without a 'pro-slavery rebellion', to this peaceful and legal revolution."

7

Marx's tactical and theoretical writings, as the preceding citations have shown, offer *some* support for both theses of reformist socialism. But not much. The starting thesis is set forth in only a few isolated, though significant, passages. The finishing thesis is less clearly and categorically affirmed than the starting thesis. Yet Bernstein, in claiming that he was revising rather than rejecting Marxian theory, could appeal to other evidence in addition to these scattered fragments. This pattern of competing systems, which Marx had sketched in outline, was elaborated and emphasized by Engels, particularly in his writings during the twelve years after Marx's death.

Marx wrote the third volume of *Capital* in 1864 and 1865 (thirty years before it was published), and his *Inaugural Address* belongs to the same period. Engels published *Anti-Dühring* some twelve years later, in 1877 and 1878; and in 1880 three chapters of this work, with minor additions, were published as *Socialism: Utopian and Scientific*. Eight years after the death of Marx, Engels wrote in 1891 his *Critique of a Draft for the Erfurt Program*. And in the year before his own death he published in 1894, with editorial comment, the third volume of *Capital*. All these writings of Engels include statements supporting the starting thesis. And one includes a clear and specific affirmation of the finishing thesis.

Marx had advanced the claim that the shift from individual to corporate enterprise represents "the transcendence of the capitalist mode of production within the capitalist mode of production." In *Anti-Dühring*—in the chapter entitled "Theoretical"—and in the third volume of *Capital*—in a comment interpolated in the chapter entitled "The Role of Credit in Capitalist Production"—Engels repeats this claim.

Marx had pointed to a tendency for joint-stock companies to develop into monopolies. In *Socialism: Utopian and Scientific*—in an addition to the chapter entitled "Theoretical" —and in the *Critique of a Draft for the Erfurt Program*, Engels points to the same tendency. But he goes beyond Marx in claiming that development of joint-stock companies into monopolies represents a transition from the unplanned production of capitalist society to "the planned production of the invading socialist society."

Marx had suggested that development of monopolies would provoke state intervention. In *Socialism: Utopian and Scientific* Engels elaborates this suggestion. The development of joint-stock companies, the development of trusts and monopolies, and the nationalization of such enterprises he describes as successive steps toward the taking over of all means of production by society. If the size of an enterprise continues to increase, he writes in the chapter already cited, "the official representative of capitalist society—the state— will ultimately have to take over its direction. The necessity for this conversion into state property first arises in the field

of transport and communication: the post-office, the tele-
graphs, the railways."

Like Marx, Engels stresses the complexities and conflicts
of these transitional developments. Neither the creation of
joint-stock companies and trusts nor the nationalization of
such enterprises, he continues, transcends capitalist ownership of the means of production. Nationalization transforms
the capitalist state into a large-scale capitalist enterprise.
"The workers remain wage-workers, proletarians. The capital
relation is not transcended but pushed to an extreme. And
at this extreme it is destroyed. State ownership of the productive forces is not the solution of this conflict; yet it provides the formal means, the levers, of that solution."

Because of such complicating factors, Engels refuses to
recognize *every* case of nationalization as a step toward
socialism. Nationalization measures must be evaluated con-
cretely, with reference to two sets of conditions: first, the
existing level of economic development, and second, the existing degree of political democracy.

In *Anti-Dühring* Engels uses the test of economic development to reject the claim that Bismarck's nationalization
of the railways represents a step towards socialism. He
argues, in the chapter entitled "Theoretical," that it was not
economic necessity that lay behind Bismarck's action, but
considerations of military efficiency, political advantage, and
private gain. Nationalization in such circumstances is not a
step toward socialism. "For only when the means of production or communication have *actually* outgrown management by joint-stock companies, when the change is economically unavoidable, does nationalization—even if carried
out by the state of today—represent an economic advance,

another step toward the taking over of all productive forces by society itself."

In every case where nationalization is economically necessary does it represent a step toward socialism? This question raises issues connected with the maximum thesis of reformism, the claim that socialist transformation of a capitalist economy can be completed without a proletarian revolution. If proletarian revolution is unavoidable, nationalization measures must be considered in terms of their effect in strengthening the power of the government against that of the people. If such measures are carried out in advance of the revolution, Engels suggests in a letter he wrote to Bebel in November 1879, they may hinder more than they help the final victory of socialism. On the other hand, it might be argued, if the transition to socialism can be accomplished peacefully, such conflicts between starting and finishing need not arise.

In his *Critique of a Draft for the Erfurt Program* Engels denies the possibility of a peaceful transition to socialism in Bismarck's Germany. Criticizing the draft for ignoring the undemocratic character of the German state, he writes: "We deceive ourselves and the Party in asserting that 'present-day society is growing into socialism' if we do not ask whether it is not consequently necessary for this society to grow out of its old political constitution—to burst, like a crab, forcibly from this old shell. Must not present-day society in Germany break the chains of its half-absolutist, unspeakably entangled, political order?"

Engels then contrasts the situation of Germany with that of contemporary democratic states. "It is conceivable that the old society can grow peacefully into the new in countries where all power is concentrated in the hands of the people's representatives, where according to the constitution anything can be done that has the support of the majority. This is the situation in democratic republics such as France and the United States. It is also the situation in monarchies such as England, where pensioning off the royal family is daily discussed in the press and the monarchy is powerless to oppose the people's will."

In all of Engels' writings this is the passage that provides strongest support for both the minimum and the maximum theses of reformist socialism. First, he agrees that in Germany the economic transition from capitalism to socialism is under way. This affirms the starting thesis. Second, he suggests that in England, the United States, and France this transition can be completed without a proletarian revolution. This affirms the finishing thesis. Why did he group France with England and the United States, twenty years after Marx had classed France with Germany in the opposing group? Because he believed that the French bureaucratic-military machine had shrunk during the intervening years? Or because he believed that stabilization of the Third Republic had weakened the independence of that machine from popular control?

Not even Bernstein has claimed that Engels repudiated the pattern of increasing misery as he repudiated the pattern of permanent revolution. During the last years of Engels' life he prophesied imminent confirmation of the theses of class polarization and increasing misery, as confidently as he and Marx had made the same prophecies more than forty years before. But alongside of the pattern of increasing misery, which continued to dominate his theoretical and tactical writings, he developed and increasingly emphasized Marx's suggestions for a pattern of competing systems. The polemics between Kautsky and Bernstein which broke out after Engels' death do not represent simply the confrontation of Marxism and Fabianism. They represent also the transformation of a latent tension in Marxian theory into an open conflict of political tendencies.

8

From the death of Engels until the present time the conflict of three tactics has recurrently divided Marxian socialists. In the period before the First World War, there was the confrontation of policies represented by Bernstein, Kautsky, and Lenin. In the period between the end of that war and the death of Lenin, there was the confrontation of policies represented by the Second International, the Vienna Union (or "Two-and-a-half International"), and the Third International. In the period of Stalin's ascendancy and Trotsky's exile, there was the confrontation of policies represented by the Second, Third, and Fourth Internationals. And in the present period, there is the confrontation of policies represented by Tito, Khrushchev, and Mao. Certainly none of the three traditions has been simply restated in successive periods, without important modifications, additions, or— notably in the case of Stalin—intermixture of opposing patterns. Certainly the character of the transition from capitalism to socialism, though the central issue, has been only one of those debated. And certainly the historical causes of these disputes must be distinguished from the theoretical principles to which the contestants have appealed. Yet to the extent that questions of theory are involved, a key to their analysis—

though hardly the analysis itself—is provided by the contrast of three patterns: minority revolution, majority revolution, and piecemeal reform.

In the present era, Communist debates over the transition from capitalism to socialism center upon three problems: first, what tactics should be adopted by Communist parties in the domestic politics of countries where these parties are not in power; second, what tactics should be adopted to construct socialism in countries where Communists are in power; and third, what tactics should be adopted by Communist countries as a group in their confrontation, diplomatic and military, with the allied imperialist powers. On each of these issues the Yugoslavian, Russian, and Chinese Communists occupy the same relative positions. The Yugoslavs advocate gradualist tactics, basing their arguments on a pattern of competing systems. The Chinese advocate tactics of "head-on collision," basing their arguments on a pattern of permanent revolution. And the Russians attempt to develop a position somewhere between the two.

What tactics should be adopted by Communist parties in the domestic politics of countries where these parties are not in power? The Program adopted in 1958 by the Communist League of Yugoslavia sets forth, in its first two chapters, a modern version of revisionism. The starting thesis is central for the argument. In imperialist countries, socialist transformation of capitalist economies is already under way; in underdeveloped countries, colonial and ex-colonial, the national liberation movement is travelling in this direction. The finishing thesis is also affirmed. Prospects for peaceful transition to socialism are now brighter than at any time in the past. To this program of modern revisionism the Chinese Communists oppose, for both imperialist and underdeveloped countries, the tactics of Leninist orthodoxy. In affirming the possibility of a parliamentary transition to socialism in the present era, first proclaimed by Khrushchev in 1956 at the Twentieth Party Congress, the Russian Communists have rejected the Leninist doctrine of minority revolution. But they have not accepted the revisionist thesis that socialist transformation of capitalist economies is already under way. What remains unclear in the Russians' position is the extent to which they believe it possible to detach the tactics of majority revolution from the predictions of class polarization and increasing misery.

What tactics should be adopted to construct socialism in countries where Communists are in power? Here the central problem is that of collectivizing agriculture. The Yugoslavs and the Poles advocate the gradualist tactics set forth by Lenin in his New Economic Policy of 1921, envisaging socialist construction in terms of a pattern of competing systems. In 1957, at the time of the *Declaration of Communist Parties of Socialist Countries,* the Russians and the Chinese joined in denouncing this "revisionist" approach, opposing to it the policy of forced collectivization adopted by Stalin in 1928— a policy of revolution from above. But their agreement ended less than a year later when the Chinese pushed beyond Stalin's example in launching the Commune movement, applying to the task of socialist construction the slogan of permanent revolution.

What tactics should be adopted by Communist countries as a group confronting, diplomatically and militarily, the allied capitalist powers? Here the central issue is the menace of atomic war. In the present situation can Communists, like Lenin in 1915, propose a program of militant struggle to spread the revolution from socialist to capitalist countries, if necessary by military means? Or have they no choice but to develop and improve the tactics of coexistence implicit in the doctrine of socialism in one country set forth by Stalin in 1924—a pattern of competing systems attacked by Trotsky under the slogan of permanent revolution?

The Chinese position on this issue is based on the thesis —first proclaimed by Mao in 1957 to the Communist leaders assembled in Moscow—that on a world scale the forces of socialism are now overwhelmingly superior to the forces of imperialism. Two tactical conclusions are drawn from this assertion of fact. First, socialist countries should not hesitate to support local wars of liberation. And second, the attitude of socialists toward a Third World War should be: We are against it but we do not fear it.

The Yugoslavs and Russians fear it. The Yugoslavs have remained outside both military blocs, seeking to organize the neutral countries in support of coexistence and disarmament. The Russians are military allies of the Chinese. But that alliance has been strained to the breaking point by the Russians' opposition to what they consider the irrationality and irresponsibility displayed by the Chinese in weighing the human costs of nuclear war.

9

The tactical disputes now shaking Marxism to its foundations reflect the central problem of our time, that fateful tension between the increasing strength of Communism and the increasing threat of atomic destruction. Is it feasible and desirable to modify Marxian tactics in order to reduce the

likelihood of a Third World War? When the Russians assert
that majority revolutions are *possible* in the present era, do
they mean that Communists everywhere should reject the
tactics of minority revolution and restrict themselves to struggling for majorities? Suppose that this is done. Suppose that
the present uneasy truce lasts for a generation, during which
the achievements of the socialist countries convince majorities
in other countries that socialism is the only answer. What
then? When the Russians assert that peaceful transitions are
possible in the present era, do they mean that Communists
everywhere should reject the tactics of majority revolution on
the ground that civil war may lead to foreign intervention?
But if Communists permanently restrict themselves to tactics
of peaceful transition, what remains of their allegiance to
the revolutionary tradition of Marx? And if they decide to
pursue such tactics, will they be able to impose that decision
upon the actual course of events?

Discussing the transition from feudalism to capitalism—
in the section of the first volume of *Capital* dealing with the
genesis of the industrial capitalist—Marx writes of the
colonial system: "It was the 'strange god' that settled himself on the altar beside the old idols of Europe and one fine
morning, with a shove and a kick, knocked them off in a
heap."

The allusion is to *Rameau's Nephew*, a work Marx
greatly admired. Diderot uses the metaphor of the strange
god to describe the tactics of the Enlightenment in struggling
to reform the civilization of eighteenth-century Europe. "The
rule of Nature and of my Trinity, against which the gates of
Hell shall not prevail—the True, which is the Father and
engenders the Good, which is the Son, from whom proceeds
the Beautiful, which is the Holy Ghost—establishes itself very

quietly. The strange god settles himself humbly on the altar beside the idol of the country. Little by little he establishes himself more firmly. Then one fine morning he gives his neighbor a shove with his elbow, and—crash!—the idol lies upon the ground." By likening the colonial system to Diderot's strange god, Marx not only points to a parallel between two patterns of development but suggests that the undermining of the old culture by the ideas of the Enlightenment reflected the undermining of the old political and economic institutions by the growth of capitalism.

In using the metaphor of the strange god was Marx also alluding to a second work, which he admired even more than that of Diderot, the *Phenomenology* of Hegel? Diderot had written that the political method exemplified by the tactics of the strange god, "which moves toward its goal without noise or bloodshed, with no martyrs made and not a single tuft of hair torn out," seemed to him the best. But Hegel, looking back on the Enlightenment from the vantage point of the Napoleonic Era, contrasts with brutal irony its intentions and its results. After quoting Diderot on the strange god, he adds: "If the infection has penetrated to every organ of spiritual life; if memory alone preserves as history the dead form of the spirit's previous incarnation, which has vanished men know not how; if the new Serpent of Wisdom, raised up before the kneeling worshippers, has painlessly shed what is only a dead skin—then will it be 'some fine morning' whose noon is not red with blood."

In our own era, is capitalism destined to play the role of the old idol and socialism that of the strange god? The crash this time might be very loud indeed.